P9-CFX-985

POPOL VUH

POPOL VUH

A SACRED BOOK OF THE MAYA

RETOLD BY

VICTOR MONTEJO

TRANSLATED BY

DAVID UNGER

•

WITH ILLUSTRATIONS BY

LUIS GARAY

A GROUNDWOOD BOOK

DOUGLAS & McINTYRE

TORONTO VANCOUVER BUFFALO

LIBRARY
FRANKLIN PIERCE COLLEGE
RINDGE, NH 03461

Text copyright © 1999 by Victor Montejo
English translation copyright © 1999 by David Unger
Illustrations copyright © 1999 by Luis Garay

All rights reserved. No part of this book may be reproduced, stored in a retrieval system or transmitted in any form or by any means, without the prior written permission of the publisher or, in the case of photocopying or other reprographic copying, a licence from CANCOPY (Canadian Reprography Collective), Toronto, Ontario.

Groundwood Books/Douglas & McIntyre
585 Bloor Street West
Toronto, Ontario M6G 1K5

Distributed in the USA by Publishers Group West
1700 Fourth Street
Berkeley, CA 94710

We acknowledge the financial support of the Canada Council for the Arts, the Ontario Arts Council and the Government of Canada through the Book Publishing Industry Development Program for our publishing activities.

Canadian Cataloguing in Publication Data

Montejo, Victor, 1951-
Popol vuh: a sacred book of the Maya

A Groundwood book.
Translation of: Popol vuj : libro sagrado de los Mayas.
ISBN 0-88899-334-X

1. Quiché mythology — Juvenile literature. 2. Quiché Indians — Religion — Juvenile literature. I. Garay, Luis, 1965- . II. Unger, David. III: Title.

CURR   F1465.P8M66 1999a   j299'.78415   C99-931365-7

Design by Michael Solomon
Printed and bound in China by Everbest Printing Co. Ltd.

Table of Contents

Introduction

The *Popol Vuh*, also known as the Sacred Book or the Bible of the Maya K'iche', is the literary gem of the indigenous people of Guatemala. Part One starts with an account of how the world was created by the will of the Heart of Heaven and the Heart of Earth, the names the Maya K'iche' give to God. The first attempt at creation failed, and the creatures were all destroyed by a flood. After this, we hear about Wuqub' K'aqix (Seven Macaws) and his very arrogant sons, Sipakna and Kab'raqan. These incidents occurred before humans were created and are mythic tales that introduce the amazing twins, Junajpu and Ixb'alanke, supernatural heroes. Part Two recounts their battles against the Underworld Lords of Xib'alb'a. Part Three describes the creation of man from corn and the fate of his descendants who populated the world. Part Four lists the line of K'iche' kings up to the arrival of the Spanish conquistadors.

The term *Popol Vuh* comes from the word Pop—which means straw mat and is also a metaphor for power. The word Vuh, or Wuj, means paper in the K'iche' language. This sacred book was perhaps written in hieroglyphic characters long before the Spaniards came to this continent. During the Spanish conquest, however, Mayan culture was brutally attacked and most of the Mayan codices were burned. The stories of the *Popol Vuh* had to be passed along orally. In 1558, the *Popol Vuh* was written down by a native who learned how to write the Mayan tongue using Latin characters. And this is how the sacred book of the Maya has been brought down to us. In 1701, Father Francisco Ximénez discovered the *Popol Vuh* manuscript in his parish church of Santo Tomás, in Chichicastenango, Guatemala, and translated it into Spanish. But Ximénez's translation was lost for more than a century. It was rediscovered in 1854 and taken from Guatemala's San Carlos University library to Europe by Abbott Brasseur de Bourbough. This cleric translated the *Popol*

Vuh into French and then sold the original manuscript to another collector named Alfonso Pinart. When Pinart died, his widow sold it to Edward E. Ayer, who brought the book back to America and deposited it in Chicago's Newberry Library, where it now rests.

The *Popol Vuh* contains mythical and historical tales that recount the origins as well as the progression of the Mayan people in Guatemala. Many of the places mentioned in the book actually exist. Starting with the creation of the world, the stories stretch over several thousand years of history of the indigenous people of the Americas. For the Maya, the teachings of the *Popol Vuh* are essential because they establish that they are the original inhabitants of the lands where they now live, thus reinforcing the idea of the origins and the identity of the indigenous people of Guatemala. In recognizing the literary and historical value of the *Popol Vuh*, we also come to recognize the power of the history, philosophy, religion and literature the early people of the Americas had. For all of us who live in the Americas, Mayan civilization, which began on this continent several thousand years ago, is a bedrock of our culture.

Victor Montejo

PART ONE
THE CREATION

●

The Beginning

THIS IS THE BEGINNING of the ancient stories of this place known as K'iche'. Here we will set down and tell the story of how all things began and of the people who live in the Mayan nation of K'iche'. Here we will also tell the remarkable story of the creation, of how things hidden in darkness were brought to light by the Creator and Maker. These are the words and the revelations given to us by our first grandfather and grandmother, whose names were Ixpiyakok and Ixmukane. These stories are now being recorded under the law of God and Christianity. We reveal this to you since the ancient book known as the *Popol Vuh*, where the story of creation and the beginning of life on this earth was written, has been lost. Remarkable was the story of how the heavens and the earth were formed and how they were divided into four parts by the Creator and Maker—he who is the father and mother of all life, the wise being who created all the beauty that exists in the sky, on the earth and in the sea.

The Creation of the Earth

IN THE BEGINNING everything was still, peaceful and silent. There was no movement because the whole expanse of the sky was empty. There were no people, no animals, no birds, fish, crabs, rocks, ravines, no mountains. Only the sky was there, completely empty. The earth still did not exist and there was nothing that could make a sound. Everything was in silence and the sea was there, motionless in the darkness. Only the Creators and Makers Tepew and Q'uk'umatz were above the waters, surrounded by light and covered with green and blue feathers. They were

13

wise men and great thinkers because they were the helpers of the Heart of Heaven, which is the name of God. Tepew and Q'uk'umatz met together. They joined their words and thoughts and decided to create the trees and the vines. By the will of the Heart of Heaven, also known as Juraqan, they created plants out of the darkness and gave life to humans.

Tepew and Q'uk'umatz went on discussing life and how to create light. They deliberated over how to lift the dawn so that it would awaken and bring the day, and who would work the earth so there would be food and sustenance.

"Let it be like this! Let the empty sky fill up! Let the waters recede and let the earth arise! Let the dawn begin, and let light cover the sky and the earth! Our creation will not be complete until human beings can walk the earth." This is what they said.

"Earth!" they cried, and at once the earth appeared. Creation was like mist or a cloud of dust, and the mountains grew forth out of the waters. All of a sudden, as if by magic, the hills and the valleys took shape, and the earth was covered with plants and trees.

When he saw this, Q'uk'umatz joyfully burst out, "Your blessings have been kind, O, Heart of Heaven, and now we can go on with our creation."

This is how the hills and valleys were made. The waters were divided to form seas and lakes. The rivers searched for their origins in the valleys when the high mountains were created. And that is how the earth was created, back when the Heart of Heaven and the Heart of Earth deliberated and joined their thoughts so that their work would be perfect.

The Creation of the Animals

THE CREATORS AND MAKERS asked themselves, "Will there only be silence and stillness beneath the tree branches and vines? It would be good if there were creatures in the trees and forests."

This is what they said, and all at once they created animals both big and small to live in the trees and forests. They created deer, birds, pumas and jaguars. Then they created serpents and poisonous snakes to be the guardians of the vines. Then the Creators and Makers gave the other animals a proper place to live.

"You, deer, shall live in the meadows, in the valleys and along the river banks. You will walk on all fours, multiply and live among the forest plants and trees."

And to the birds they said, "You, birds, shall live in the trees, among the vines. There you will build your nests and multiply." This is what they said to the deer and the birds, and to all the other animals who were given their proper place to live on the earth.

After creating the birds and the animals, the Creators and Makers said, "Talk, cry out, sing, each according to what you are. Praise us and thank us for creating you. Invoke the names of the Creators and Makers, who are the fathers and mothers of all life. Thank our forefather who is God, the Heart of Heaven and the Heart of Earth." This is what they said, but they were not able to get the animals to speak like humans. The animals tried to speak, but instead they squawked, chattered, roared and howled. Each creature made a different sound or cry.

When the Creators and Makers realized that the animals could not speak, they said, "Since you are unable to speak, we have changed our minds. You will live just as you are in the valleys and in the forests. We have decided to do this since you are unable to speak and praise us for having created you. We will go on with our work until we have made a creature who is respectful and able to sing our praises. From now on your flesh will be consumed and eaten. This is your fate." They said this to the animals, both big and small, who lived on the earth. From then on, the flesh of animals could be eaten.

The First Creation of Humans: The Clay People

ONCE AGAIN, THE CREATORS AND MAKERS TRIED to create humans. "Let's try again! The sun is about to rise and we need to prepare the one who will nourish us. How else can we be sure that we will be invoked and remembered on earth? We tried with the first creatures, but they wouldn't

honor us. Let's try again to make intelligent and respectful creatures who will sustain us and sing our praises."

And so they began creating man. The Creators and Makers made a body out of clay, but they soon realized that they hadn't done a good job, for almost at once their man began to fall apart. His body was mushy and weak and could not move. He could not lift his arms or even see. At first he could speak, but he had no feelings and no understanding of things. He began to dissolve in water and could not walk or multiply.

The Creators and Makers decided to destroy their creation, and once again they gathered together. "How can we create the perfect creature who will honor us and sing our praises?"

The Second Creation of Humans: The Wooden People

So THEY ASKED THEIR ELDERS—the first grandfather and grandmother, Ixpiyakok and Ixmukane—for help. "Let's try again, try once more to create man," the Creators and Makers said to Ixpiyakok, grandfather of day, and to Ixmukane, grandmother of the sunrise.

"Let's make a human who will nourish us, who will pray to us, invoke our names and remember us. Discuss it among yourselves, Grandmother and Grandfather. Use the powers of the corn kernels and tz'ite' seeds to decide the substance for the body of man."

So Ixpiyakok and Ixmukane used their powers of divination and said to the corn kernels and the tz'ite' seeds, "Discuss it among yourselves and give us your answer. Speak clearly, for we are listening to you. Tell us if it would be wise to carve him out of wood. Tell us if the wooden people would nourish and honor us when the sun rises and lights the face of the earth."

They soon received a reply. "The wooden people will be good; they will be able to speak and have many children," said the corn kernels and the tz'ite' seeds.

The Creators and Makers said, "So be it." And all at once the wooden people were created. They resembled humans, talked like people and multiplied on the earth. They produced sons and daughters, but neither had souls nor the gift of reason. They did not remember their Creators and Makers and wandered about aimlessly, crawling along the earth. And so they fell into disgrace because they did not remember their Creators and Makers. Even though they could talk, their faces were hard and rigid with no expression. Their hands and feet were not firm because they lacked both blood and flesh. These were the first humans to walk the earth in large numbers.

By the will of the Heart of Heaven, a flood destroyed the wooden people. The body of the first man was made of tz'ite' wood and the body of the first woman was made of espadaña reeds. But these first creatures were condemned to destruction because they could not think and could not communicate with their Creators and Makers. A boiling, fine rain fell from the sky and Xek'otk'owach the turkey buzzard flew down and pecked out their eyes. Kamalotz the vampire bat flew down and lopped off their heads. And finally Kotz'b'alam the jaguar arrived and swallowed them up. Tukum b'alam the puma also took part in the destruction and crushed their bones so he could suck out the marrow. And this is how these creatures were punished for not remembering their Creator, the Heart of Heaven, also known as Juraqan. For this reason the sky darkened and a black rain began to fall day and night for a very long time. And all creatures, both big and small, came to punish the wooden people. Even the sticks and stones began beating them in the face. Their tools, their water jugs, tortilla griddles, dishes, cooking pots, dogs, even their grinding stones rose up to punish them.

"You caused us much harm and you ate our flesh. Now we are going to eat you in return," said their dogs and the other creatures.

The grinding stones complained, "You tortured us day and night. Each morning, holi, holi, huki, huki, you grind corn right over our faces. Now that you have fallen into disgrace you will learn what it feels like to be ground. We are going to change your flesh into dust."

The dogs then added, "Why didn't you feed us? We lay very patiently at your feet waiting for something to eat, but you screamed and chased us out of the house. You always kept a stick nearby to beat us if we came too close to you while you ate. You treated us like this because we could not talk and complain about your cruel ways. Why didn't you care? Why did you think only of yourselves and your own future? Now we will destroy you, crush you with our teeth."

Even the tortilla griddles and the cooking pots complained. "You brought us much pain and suffering. Our faces are black as coal because you left us burning over the fire. Now it's your turn to suffer," they said to the wooden people as they began striking their faces.

The wooden people ran off in all directions. They tried to climb onto the house tops, but the roofs collapsed and flung them to the ground. They climbed up the trees, but the trees shook their limbs, tossing them back down. They even tried to hide in caves, but the caves blocked off their entrances so that they couldn't get inside.

This is how the wooden people were destroyed. It's said that the monkeys now living in the trees are their offspring. This is why monkeys look like people. They are the survivors of the generation of wooden people made by the Creators and Makers.

PART TWO

THE AMAZING TWINS

● ●

The Pride of Wuqub' K'aqix (Seven Macaws)

These are the stories of what happened before the creation of mankind, when the demi-gods and the supernatural beings created by the Heart of Heaven and the Heart of Earth quarreled among themselves.

THE SKY AND THE EARTH NOW EXISTED, but there was still no sun, no moon. Wuqub' K'aqix was there, however, bragging about himself. "I am the greatest thing that has ever been created. I am the sun, the moon— great is my splendor. My eyes are made of silver and glow like precious gems. When I walk, the earth lights up before me. I am both the sun and the moon because my eyes can see a very long way off."

Actually, Wuqub' K'aqix was neither the sun nor the moon. He only bragged about his feathers and his wealth. Since light had not been created, Wuqub' K'aqix claimed he was the sun and the moon. His one goal was to grow more powerful and rule over the earth.

So the amazing twin demi-gods, Junajpu and Ixb'alankc, decided to punish Wuqub' K'aqix for his pride.

"There's no room for pride when man doesn't even exist yet. We will shoot him with our blowguns and make him sick. This will put an end to his wealth, power and pride."

Wuqub' K'aqix had two sons, Sipakna and Kab'raqan, and their mother's name was Chimalmat. Sipakna was busy making the mountains and volcanoes grow while Kab'raqan shook the earth, setting off earthquakes. Wuqub' K'aqix and his two sons proclaimed their power and their pride, saying, "Listen, all of you, I am the sun!"

"I'm the one who created the mountains!" said Sipakna.

"I'm the one who shakes the sky and makes the earth quake!" said Kab'raqan.

That's how Wuqub' K'aqix and his sons boasted, which displeased the twins Junajpu and Ixb'alanke. All this happened before our very first ancestors were created.

Wuqub' K'aqix came every day to eat fruit from the nance tree, and that's where the twins waited for him with their blowguns. The boys hid themselves in the undergrowth and aimed at Wuqub' K'aqix, who had climbed up the tree. Junajpu fired off a pellet with his blowgun and struck him in the jaw. Wuqub' K'aqix tumbled out of the tree and landed on the ground screaming.

Junajpu ran over to capture Wuqub' K'aqix, but Wuqub' yanked off one of his arms. Wuqub' K'aqix rushed home crying, but with Junajpu's arm in his hand.

"What happened?" asked his wife, Chimalmat.

"Those two evil boys shot me with their blowguns and dislocated my jaw. But look here. I yanked off one of their arms and we can broil it over the fire. I'm sure they'll come here to get it back."

The twins considered what to do and decided to ask two gray-haired, hunchbacked elders for help. The old man was Saqi Nim Ak' and the old woman was Saqi Nima Tz'i'.

The boys said to the elders, "Come with us to Wuqub' K'aqix's house. You can tell him that we're your grandchildren and that our parents are dead. Tell him we follow you where ever you go and that your job is to dig out the worm that causes toothaches."

The elders agreed and they set off, with the boys running and skipping after them. When they reached Wuqub' K'aqix's house, they saw him stretched out in his throne, crying in pain.

As soon as Wuqub' K'aqix saw the elders, he asked them, "Where are you from, old ones? Are these your children?"

"We're looking for work," the elders replied. "You see, we are healers and these are our grandchildren. We give them part of the food we are able to get."

"What kind of healers are you? Have pity on me," Wuqub' K'aqix implored.

"Sir, we pull out the worm that makes teeth ache. We also care for eyes and reset bones."

"Great! I want you to heal my teeth because they ache day and night. Two wicked boys shot me in the jaw with a pellet and now I can neither eat nor sleep."

"All right. A worm must be the cause of your pain. We'll pull out your teeth and put new ones in their place," the elders replied.

"I don't want you to pull out my teeth because their brightness makes me feel important and powerful," Wuqub' K'aqix answered.

"Don't worry. We'll put others in."

So the elders took out Wuqub' K'aqix's teeth and put kernels of white corn in their place. This is how Wuqub' K'aqix's light dimmed and he lost his power. They also plucked the pupils out of his eyes. That's how he lost his light and his greatness. The elders defeated Wuqub' K'aqix by stripping him of his precious gems. Junajpu recovered his arm and Wuqub' K'aqix went down in defeat, according to the will of the Heart of Heaven.

Sipakna the Mountain Giant

AND NOW THIS IS WHAT HAPPENED to Sipakna, Wuqub' K'aqix's oldest son. Sipakna was a show-off who said, "I created the mountains." While he bathed in the river waters, four hundred boys passed by dragging a huge beam to be used as a post for their hut.

"Hello, boys. What are you doing?" Sipakna asked.

"We're trying to lift this log, but can't."

"I'll pick it up and carry it for you. What do you want it for?"

"As a beam to hold up our new hut," the boys answered.

Sipakna lifted the log and carried it on his shoulders to the front of the hut. There the boys asked him, "Do you have a mother and a father?"

"I do not," Sipakna replied.

"In that case, why don't you stay with us? Tomorrow we'll go looking for another log for our hut."

"All right," Sipakna said.

The boys came together to discuss Sipakna.

"What'll we do with him? He's too strong. He lifted the post all by himself and that's not good. Now we'll have to kill him. Let's dig a very deep hole and then ask him to jump in and dig it deeper. When Sipakna is down there, we'll heave a huge log on top of him and crush him to death."

The four hundred boys dug a huge hole. When they had finished, they called Sipakna. "Can you help us? The hole's so deep now that we can't even reach the bottom."

"Very well," said Sipakna, and he jumped into the hole to deepen it.

"Have you finished yet?" they shouted down to him.

"I've almost done it," he called up from the bottom.

Actually, Sipakna was digging a tunnel on the side to get away. He had heard the boys whispering that they wanted to kill him.

When Sipakna was safe, he called up to the boys and told them he had finished digging. As soon as the boys heard his voice, they threw down the huge log, which made an enormous noise as it tumbled into the hole. The four hundred boys stood perfectly quiet. Just then Sipakna let out a single cry from the bottom of the hole.

The boys congratulated one another. "Our plan worked. If he had stayed with us, he would have caused us much harm because he's so strong and powerful. Now we can make our chicha and let it ferment for three days. On the third day we will have a party and drink it. Tomorrow and the day after we'll keep a lookout for ants coming out of the hole with chunks of Sipakna's rotting body. That's how we can tell he's really dead and we can get drunk and feel safe."

Sipakna could hear this from his hideout down below. He tore out his hair and his nails with his teeth and gave them to the ants. When the four hundred boys saw the ants coming out of the hole with pieces of Sipakna's nails and hair, they cried joyfully, "Our plan worked! Now we know for sure that the cruel one is dead."

The boys began their party and drank so much chicha they were drunk. They didn't hear Sipakna climb out of the hole and topple the hut on top of them. And this is how the four hundred boys were crushed when the roof of their hut collapsed on them. Once dead, they rose up into the sky and became the stars of the Pleiades constellation—Motz, meaning group or crowd in the Mayan language.

The Death of Sipakna

NOW YOU SHALL HEAR how Sipakna died at the hands of the amazing twins Junajpu and Ixb'alanke, who were furious when they heard about the death of the four hundred boys.

Sipakna lived on the banks of a river, where he survived on fish and crabs. The twins decided to trick Sipakna by building a huge false crab. They used ek' flowers to make it and then used a thin red flagstone for the shell. They placed the crab in a cave at the foot of Meaván Mountain.

Junajpu and Ixb'alanke went to look for Sipakna and found him on the banks of a river.

"Where are you going?"

"Nowhere in particular. I'm just hunting for food," Sipakna replied.

"And what do you eat?"

"Just fish and crab, but there are none here. I haven't eaten for two days and I am very hungry."

"Down at the bottom of the ravine we saw a huge crab that would make a fine feast. We tried to catch it, but it bit us. We're scared of it," Junajpu and Ixb'alanke said.

"Please have pity on me and show me where I can find this crab," Sipakna pleaded.

"We're too scared to go back to that place. You can't miss it if you go by yourself. Walk upriver and there it'll be, scuttling about in a cave at the foot of the hill."

"Alas! I won't be able to find it without your help. If you come with me, I'll take you to a place where there are lots of birds. You can use your blow-guns to kill them."

"We'll show you the spot if you really want to catch the crab. We don't want to go back just for the fun of it. You'll have to crawl into the cave hole face down to capture it," they told him. And that's how they got Sipakna to go to where they had set the trap.

"Very well," said Sipakna, and he followed the boys down to the ravine at the foot of the hill. There he saw the crab moving from side to side, with its deep red shell. Sipakna crawled into the hole and tried to grab it. But the crab moved farther back inside the cave.

"I can almost taste it in my mouth," Sipakna repeated hungrily.

When Sipakna crawled out of the cave a little while later, the boys asked, "Have you caught it yet?"

"No, it just scurries farther back. I'll have better luck if I crawl in face up, on my back, and grab it."

So Sipakna went into the cave on his back. When only his feet remained outside, the cave collapsed on his chest, pinning him down. Sipakna did not make it out of the cave alive, and they say that he turned to stone.

That is how Sipakna was defeated at the foot of Meavan Mountain by Junajpu and Ixb'alanke.

Kab'raqan, Lord of the Earthquakes

THE THIRD BRAGGART WAS KAB'RAQAN, the second son of Wuqub' K'aqix. "I'm the one who topples mountains," he boasted.

So the Heart of Heaven told Junajpu and Ixb'alanke that Kab'raqan had to be destroyed as well.

"Wuqub' K'aqix's other son has to be humbled. This bragging and showing off of his powers on earth is not right. This is my will," said the Heart of Heaven.

"Very well," the young boys said. "We know that you, Heart of Heaven, come first. You are everything great, powerful and peaceful."

In the meantime, Kab'raqan was busy shaking the mountains. By simply dropping his feet on the ground, he toppled mountains, both big and small.

When the boys ran into him, they asked, "Where are you going, young man?"

"Nowhere in particular. I'm just enjoying myself by destroying mountains," answered Kab'raqan. "I'm going to do this forever and ever. And who are you? Why have you come this far?"

"We have no names. All we do is shoot birds with our blowguns. We are very poor and have no possessions. Our only pleasure is walking up and down mountains, big and small, looking for birds. There, where the sun rises, we've just seen a huge mountain—in fact, the tallest mountain of them all. It is so high that we were not able to climb it to hunt for birds. Is it true that you can knock down all the mountains?" Junajpu and Ixb'alanke asked.

"Have you really seen such a tall mountain? Where is it? I will knock it down to the ground right away."

"The mountain is over there, where the sun rises," they told him.

"Very well then. Just show me the way and I will follow you."

"It would be better if you walked between us. One of us on your right and the other on the left. We want to shoot birds with our blowguns as we go along and this way they won't be scared off."

They walked happily down the path while Junajpu and Ixb'alanke went along killing birds with their blowguns. They brought down the birds with their breath, not needing pellets. Kab'raqan was truly amazed at their skill. They stopped in the forest and built a fire to roast the birds. They smeared tizate, a white chalk-like powder, on one of the birds. "The smell of the birds as they roast will stir Kab'raqan's appetite. The tizate-covered bird will be Kab'raqan's downfall and he will faint, defeated by our power," the boys said to one another.

In the meantime, the birds roasted slowly, while the fat dripping from them gave off a tempting aroma. Kab'raqan was so anxious to taste them that his mouth started to water. "This meal looks delicious. I need to have a little bit," he said.

So the boys gave him the bird smeared with white powder. When Kab'raqan had finished eating the bird, they continued on their way toward the mountain in the east. But Kab'raqan started to feel weak, and his hands and feet began to lose their mobility. He was now so drained of strength that he could do nothing to the mountains. It was easy for the boys to tie up his hands and feet and throw him to the ground. Kab'raqan soon died and they buried him on the spot. And that is how Junajpu and Ixb'alanke defeated Kab'raqan simply by using their magic powers.

Jun Junajpu and Wuqub' Junajpu, the First Set of Twins, and the Xib'alb'a Lords

Now we will go back to the story of Jun Junajpu and Wuqub' Junajpu, the amazing twins' father and uncle who were also twins. These were the sons of the elders Ixpiyakok and Ixmukane. Jun Junajpu had two elder sons named Jun B'atz' and Jun Ch'owem, who were great musicians, painters and sculptors.

JUN JUNAJPU AND WUQUB' JUNAJPU spent all their time playing ball every single day. One day Jun Kame and Wuqub' Kame, the Lords of Xib'alb'a who were napping in the Underworld, heard them playing ball.

"What's going on up there on the earth?" they called out angrily. "Who's responsible for this racket? Have them brought here and we'll challenge them to a ball game. They've lost respect for us and are making too much noise above our heads."

The Lords of Xib'alb'a gathered in council to decide what to do.

Jun Kame and Wuqub' Kame were the supreme lawmakers of Xib'alb'a. The other lords present had different roles. Xikiripat and Kuchumakik' made people vomit blood. Ajalpuj and Ajalk'ana' made welts rise up on the skin of people. Chamiyab'aq and Chamiyajom made people lose weight. Ajalmes and Ajaltoq'ob' caused heart attacks and sudden death. Kik'xik' and Patan caused accidents on the roadways.

They all came together to torture and punish Jun Junajpu and Wuqub' Junajpu. The Lords of Xib'alb'a sent owls—their messengers—to summon the ball players.

"Go and convince them to come and play ball with us. Have them bring their equipment, their balls and their gear," they told the owls.

The four messenger owls left Xib'alb'a and very quickly arrived at the ball court where Jun Junajpu and Wuqub' Junajpu were playing.

After hearing the request, the twins answered, "Very well, we will play ball in Xib'alb'a. But first we need to say goodbye to our grandmother."

So they went to say goodbye to their grandmother. Before leaving, Jun Junajpu instructed his sons, Jun B'atz' and Jun Ch'owem, "Keep yourselves busy playing the flute, singing, painting and sculpting. Keep the fire burning inside the hut and keep grandmother's heart happy, for she will surely be sad."

Then they left with the owls and went down a very steep ladder to Xib'alb'a. They easily crossed several underground rivers until they reached a crossroads where they would be defeated. Each road was a different color—red, black, white and yellow. The black road was the right path—the one they took.

They reached the hall of the Lords of Xib'alb'a, but in their place the lords had set up two wooden puppets.

Jun Junajpu and Wuqub' Junajpu addressed them. "Greetings, Jun Kame and Wuqub' Kame."

The Lords of Xib'alb'a laughed, because the two young men were greeting wooden puppets.

"Sit down and rest," said the Lords of Xib'alb'a.

The twins sat down. They immediately shot up because the stone bench was burning hot. The Lords of Xib'alb'a laughed once more; the two brothers were not very smart and didn't know how to avoid dangers.

Then they were put in the Dark House. There was nothing but darkness inside. They were each given an ocote torch and a cigar. "Light the torch and your cigar, but tomorrow you will have to return them to us whole. Do not let the torch or cigar burn up."

Jun Junajpu and Wuqub' Junajpu lit their cigars and torches. In the morning, they were asked to give them back, but they had used them up during the night. The lords decided to destroy them because they had failed the Xib'alb'a test.

Jun Junajpu's head was carried on a stick and placed on the branch of a tree that had never borne fruit. It was on the road to Xib'alb'a. As soon as the head was put on the tree, round calabashes sprouted all over the branches and the head could not be distinguished from the other fruit. Then the Lords of Xib'alb'a ordered that no one come near the forbidden tree.

"Don't anyone ever come to pick these fruits," the Lords of Xib'alb'a commanded.

Princess Ixkik'

PRINCESS IXKIK', THE DAUGHTER OF KUCHUMAKIK', heard the story of the forbidden fruit tree and wanted to go and see it. When Ixkik' reached the foot of the tree, she saw the round gourds and wanted to touch them.

"Am I going to die if I touch them?" she asked herself.

Just then the skull among the branches spoke to the young woman. "What you think are fruits are actually skulls. Are you sure you want to pick them?"

"Yes, I want them," said the princess.

"Very well. Just stretch out your right hand." The young woman reached for the skull. At that moment the skull spat right into the princess's hand. Surprised, she looked down at her palm, but the saliva had already evaporated.

"My offspring is in the spit. Go back up to the earth and you will not die. Trust in my word," said the skull in the tree.

And this is how Princess Ixkik' was made pregnant by the saliva. And this is how the amazing twins Junajpu and Ixb'alanke were created. They are the very same ones who destroyed Wuqub' K'aqix, Kab'raqan and Sipakna. Kuchumakik', the father of the princess, noticed that she was pregnant and grew very angry.

He brought together the other Lords of Xib'alb'a and told them, "My daughter is pregnant. She has dishonored us."

"Make her confess whose child she is carrying. If she doesn't tell the truth, she will be sacrificed," the lords said.

"Daughter of mine, whose child are you carrying in your belly?" Kuchumakik' asked.

"No one's. I have known no man," she replied.

Kuchumakik' grew angry and told the messenger owls to put her to death and bring back her heart as proof that they had followed his orders. The owls took her and were about to kill her with a flint knife.

"Don't kill me. I have done nothing wrong," said the young woman.

"What can we substitute for your heart? The lords have asked us to bring it back so that they can burn it as an offering."

"Why don't you take the sap from that tree and place it inside a gourd," she suggested.

They tapped the chik'te' tree and the sap thickened in the shape of a heart.

"Very well. We will take this heart made of tree sap to the lords. You can go on your way back to earth," said the owls.

The Lords of Xib'alb'a were waiting for the owls to return.

"Well," said Jun Kame. "Let's see the heart you brought us."

The heart appeared red and full of blood, though it was really tree sap.

"Light the fire and place the heart on the coals," Jun Kame ordered.

The owls tossed the heart into the fire and immediately the lords smelled the aroma of the heart burning on the coals. While the Lords of Xib'alb'a were gathered together, the owls flew away and went up to earth to serve the princess. And this is how Princess Ixkik' triumphed over the Lords of Xib'alb'a.

Princess Ixkik' Passes the Test

JUN B'ATZ' AND JUN CH'OWEM were visiting their grandmother when Princess Ixkik' arrived at Jun Junajpu's hut, whose skull had impregnated the young woman.

The princess greeted the grandmother. "Here I am, dear mother. I am your daughter-in-law."

"Get out of here! You will never be my daughter-in-law," the old woman shouted.

Princess Ixkik' insisted that she was carrying the sons of Jun Junajpu in her belly, so the grandmother devised a test.

"If you are truly my daughter-in-law, bring back a sack of corn ears from the field."

"Very well," said the princess, and she went to get corn from the field of Jun B'atz' and Jun Ch'owem. Instead she only found one corn plant, nothing else.

The princess grew sad to find no corn to fill the sack. She then invoked the Corn Spirit. "Ixtoj, Ixq'anil, Ixkakaw. You who cook corn and you who are the Corn Spirit please help me."

She then cut the red hairs from the only ear of corn she found and stuffed them in the sack. The sack miraculously filled up, and the pack animals carried the sack to the grandmother's hut.

The grandmother believed that the princess had harvested the only corn plant, but no, it was still standing there. So the grandmother accepted the princess as her daughter-in-law.

"This is proof enough that you are my daughter-in-law. Let's see if those in your belly will also turn out to be wisemen," the grandmother said.

The Birth of Junajpu and Ixb'alanke, the Amazing Twins

WHEN THE BIRTH DATE ARRIVED, Ixkik' delivered the twins Junajpu and Ixb'alanke. The grandmother grew angry at hearing them cry day and night.

"They cry too much. Throw them out," the grandmother said.

Jun B'atz' and Jun Ch'owem put them on an ant hill, but there the newborns slept peacefully. They placed them on thorns, but they continued to sleep calmly. Their half-brothers Jun B'atz' and Jun Ch'owem wanted them to die. They were jealous of the newborn twins.

Junajpu and Ixb'alanke grew, and every day they practiced shooting birds with their blowguns. Jun B'atz' and Jun Ch'owem, along with the grandmother, neglected them and would not feed them. In spite of their bad treatment, the twins were not angry and suffered silently. Whenever they brought home birds, Jun B'atz' and Jun Ch'owem would eat them all instead of sharing them with the twins.

But once Junajpu and Ixb'alanke returned without a single bird.

"Why haven't you brought us any birds today?" asked the grandmother angrily.

"The dead birds are trapped in the tree branches and we can't get them down. Our older brothers should come with us to bring the birds down from the tree," they replied.

"Very well. We will go with you tomorrow to fetch them," said the older brothers.

Junajpu and Ixb'alanke wanted to run away from their brothers because they were so mean.

The following day, when they reached the foot of the tree, they found many birds hanging in the tree but not a single one on the ground.

"Climb up and bring down the birds," said the twins.

"Very well," said the older brothers, climbing. While they were up in the tree, it began to grow taller and its trunk thickened. Jun B'atz' and Jun Ch'owem wanted to climb down, but were not able to.

"Brothers, we're afraid to come down. The tree is much too tall," they called down from above.

"Loosen your sashes and have them hang down from your waist so it'll be easier for you to get down," said the twins.

Jun B'atz' and Jun Ch'owem loosened their sashes from their waists so that the ends hung behind them. This is how their sashes became tails and they were turned into monkeys. They ran at once into the jungle, making faces and swinging from the tree branches.

Junajpu and Ixb'alanke returned home and told their grandmother, "Something's happened to our brothers. They've been turned into monkeys."

The grandmother grew sad. She asked the twins to take her to see them.

"Our brothers will come back, but you must not laugh, Grandmother."

They went into the jungle, playing their flutes and singing. Jun B'atz' and Jun Ch'owem finally arrived dancing. When the grandmother saw the faces they made, she burst out laughing. The two monkeys simply scampered away.

"See, Grandma, they've fled into the jungle because you laughed at them. We'll play our flute and drums and see if they come back, but you must pass the test and not laugh," they told her. They played their instruments and Jun B'atz' and Jun Ch'owem returned making faces, but the grandmother laughed once more. The twins warned her again. "This will be the last time, Grandma. If you burst out laughing again, they will flee into the jungle, never to return."

They started to play the flute right away. Jun B'atz' and Jun Ch'owem came back, dancing all the way to the house. They spun around, making so many faces that the grandmother once again let out a great burst of laughter. The two monkeys ran back into the jungle as fast as they could, never to return.

And that is how Jun B'atz' and Jun Ch'owem were turned into monkeys and defeated.

How the Amazing Twins Became Ball Players

JUNAJPU AND IXB'ALANKE BEGAN WORKING in the corn field. As soon as they sank their picks into the soil, the picks would turn over the earth by themselves. This is also how they chopped down trees. They'd drive their axes into the trunks and the trees would fall down without the twins even lifting a finger. They asked the dove Ixmukur to keep watch and begin cooing as soon as their grandmother appeared. When she arrived, they rubbed dirt into their hands so it seemed as if they had been working. Even though their tools did all the work, they returned home to rest in the afternoons. When they returned to the field the following day, they were surprised to see that the trees were all standing once again.

"Who has pulled this trick on us?" they asked.

Animals, both big and small, had done this to them: the puma, the jaguar, the deer, the rabbit, the bobcat, the coyote, the wild hog, the pizote and the birds. These were the animals that had made the jungle rise back up in a single night.

The following day the boys went back to chop down trees and till the earth. But the pick and the ax did the work while the twins hunted birds with their blowguns. At sundown, the twins decided to hide themselves in the brush to surprise those adversaries who undid their efforts.

The animals, big and small, arrived in the middle of the night. Each spoke his very own language. "Get up, trees! Vines, return to your places!"

The puma and the jaguar were the first animals to appear, but the twins could not catch them. When the deer and the rabbit passed by, they grabbed them by their tails, but the tails broke off in their hands—this is why deer and rabbits now have short tails. The bobcat, the coyote, the wild hog and the pizote rushed by, and the twins could not catch them. The mouse ran by last of all, and the twins were able to catch him.

They squeezed the mouse's throat and burned his tail. Since then mice have bulging eyes and hairless tails.

As the mouse was being choked to death, he begged, "Please don't kill me. After all, your job is not to work the soil."

"Speak up! What are you trying to tell us?" the twins asked.

"Let me go. Give me something to eat and I'll tell you what I mean."

"Talk first and then we will feed you," they replied.

"Very well. You should know that your father Jun Junajpu and his brother Wuqub' Junajpu were ball players who died in Xib'alb'a. Your grandmother doesn't want to give you the equipment for ball playing, which she has hidden on the roof of the hut."

The young men were very happy to hear this and they fed the mouse.

"Thanks for giving us this information. From now on, corn, chili seeds, beans and cacao seeds will be the food of mice. You will also be able to eat any food that is either stored or forgotten," said the twins.

Then Junajpu and Ixb'alanke took the mouse back home and hid him under the roof so that the grandmother wouldn't see him. They then told her they were very hungry and wanted to eat food with chili.

While they ate, the twins said, "We're very thirsty, Grandma. Go and get us water from the spring."

The grandmother took her jug to get water from the spring. In the meantime, the mouse began to gnaw on the ropes wrapped around the ball-game equipment.

They tried to figure out a way to delay their grandmother's return. They sent Xa'n the mosquito to make a hole in the grandmother's jug. The mosquito bit into it and the water started flowing out of the hole. The grandmother was forced to repair it.

The mouse had just about finished gnawing on the ropes when they sent their mother Ixkik' to see what was taking their grandmother so long. Ixkik' left the hut and went to see the grandmother. At that moment the mouse finished gnawing on the cords and the rubber ball, the wrist guards and the knee pads dropped to the ground. The twins picked up the equipment and hid it by the footpath. Then they joined their grandmother and Ixkik', who were both busy patching the hole made by the mosquito.

The twins repaired the jug and everyone returned home. This is how Junajpu and Ixb'alanke found the rubber ball hidden in the roof of the hut.

The Messenger Creatures

THE TWINS WENT OFF HAPPILY to the court where they could play ball. This was the same place where Jun Junajpu and Wuqub' Junajpu used to play. Once more the Lords of Xib'alb'a heard the footsteps and shouts of ball players overhead, and they were annoyed. They sent their messengers at once to bring back the boys.

The messengers left word with the grandmother, as the boys were off playing ball.

"Have the young men come down and play ball against the Lords of Xib'alb'a. They are expected within seven days." Saying this, the owls flew off.

"Very well," said the grandmother. "I will give them the message."

The grandmother grew sad because this was how her sons Jun Junajpu and Wuqub' Junajpu had been called to Xib'alb'a, never to return. "Who should I send to keep the boys from playing in the ball court?"

While she was wondering aloud, a louse fell out of her head and onto her lap. She lifted up the louse and laid him in the palm of her hand. "Go and get my grandchildren and tell them that the Lords of Xib'alb'a want them to go and play ball. Tell them to come at once since they only have seven days to get down there," the grandmother said.

The louse flew off at once to warn them. On the way there, he ran into Tamasul, the toad.

"Where are you off to?" asked the toad.

"I'm looking for the boys to give them a message," the louse answered.

"Very well, but you'd better hurry up. I'll swallow you and this way we'll get there faster," the toad said.

The toad swallowed the louse and started hopping away leisurely. Soon the toad ran into Sakikas, the snake.

"Where are you off to, Tamasul?" the snake inquired.

"I'm off to find the young men. I have a message for them inside my belly," the toad said.

"Very well, but you are moving so slowly. I can swallow you and we'll get there faster."

The snake gulped down the toad and started to slither away very rapidly. A little farther on, the snake met up with Wak, the sparrow hawk, who swallowed the snake and flew off to the ball court where the boys were playing.

The sparrow hawk called out to them, "Vak-ko, vak-ko!" The twins grabbed their blowguns, aimed at the sparrow hawk and a pellet hit him in the eye. The sparrow hawk spun around in the sky and fell to the ground. Immediately the boys ran to pick it up.

"What are you up to here?" they asked.

"I have a message for you, but first heal my eye," the sparrow hawk asked.

The boys healed the eye and then ordered him to relay the message. "Speak up now," they commanded.

Just then the hawk spit up a huge snake.

"Speak up!" they said to the snake.

"Very well," said the snake, and he vomited up the toad.

"Speak up. What's the message?" they asked.

"The message is in my stomach," the toad answered.

Then the toad wanted to throw up the louse but wasn't able to. His mouth just filled up with saliva, his eyes bulging from the effort, but nothing happened. The boys kicked the toad and pulled open his mouth and dug out the louse, which was stuck under the tongue. Since then toads have had big mouths.

"Speak up," they said.

The louse finally gave them the message. "Your grandmother sent me to tell you that the messengers of Jun Kame and Wuqub' Kame have come to challenge you to a ball game in Xib'alb'a. You have seven days to get there. This is the message from your grandmother."

The boys returned home to get their equipment ready for the game.

"We're off, Grandma. We only came to say goodbye. But we will leave you a sign as proof of our luck. We will plant a corn stalk here in the middle of the hut. If it withers, it means we are dead, but if it sprouts, we are alive," the boys said.

So Junajpu and Ixb'alanke both planted corn stalks in the middle of the hut. They planted them in dry earth.

The Journey to Xib'alb'a

JUNAJPU AND IXB'ALANKE SET OFF on the road to Xib'alb'a. They easily crossed several underground rivers. They should have been destroyed when they reached the river of blood, but they crossed it by floating across on top of their blowguns. They knew all about the black, white, red and yellow roads to Xib'alb'a. Before reaching the lords, the twins sent off Xa'n, the mosquito, to scout ahead.

"Bite each lord, one at a time, until you've bitten them all down to the last one. This is your job: to suck out the blood of travelers on the roadways," they told the mosquito.

The mosquito went down the black road. The Lords of Xib'alb'a were seated there, waiting for the arrival of the boys. The mosquito bit the first lord, who said nothing. He bit the second lord and this one also said nothing. They were only wooden puppets keeping watch. The mosquito stung the third lord who finally cried, "Ow!" when he felt the bite.

"What's wrong with you, Jun Kame?" asked the fourth lord.

"Ouch!" screamed the fourth lord.

"What's bitten you, Wuqub' Kame?" asked the fifth lord.

"Ouch!" shouted the fifth lord.

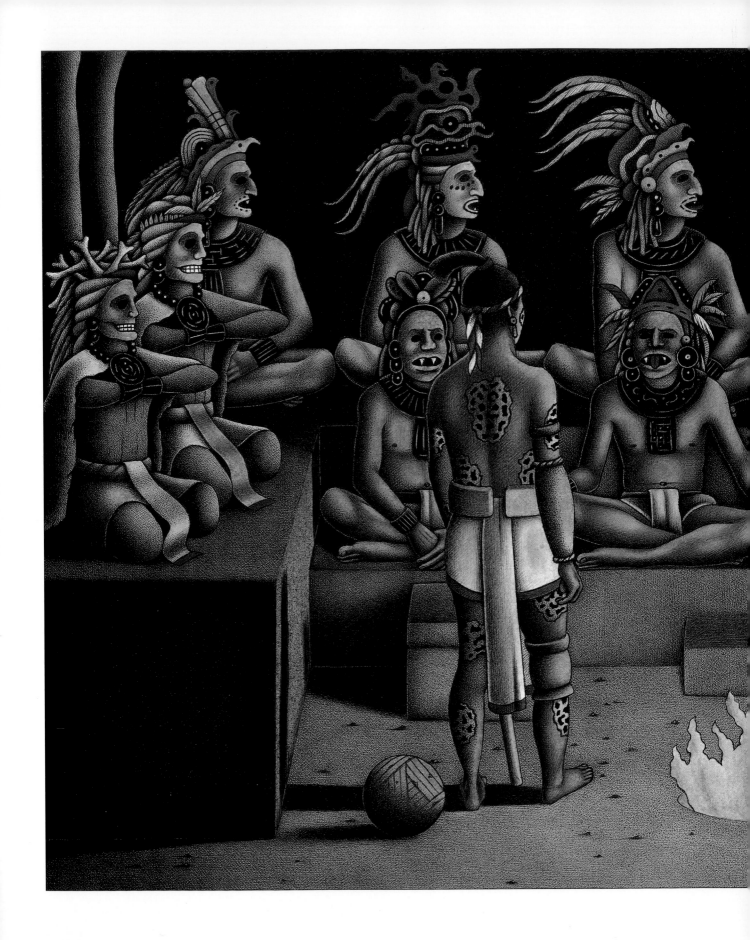

"What's bitten you, Kuchumakik'?" asked the sixth lord.

"Ouch!" yelled the sixth lord.

"What's bitten you, Xikiripat?" asked the seventh lord.

"Ouch!" cried the seventh lord.

And so it went.

"What's bitten you, Ajalpuj?"

"What's bitten you, Chamiyab'aq?"

"What's bitten you, Ajalk'ana'?"

"What's bitten you, Chamiyajom?"

"What's bitten you, Patan?"

"What's bitten you, Kik'xik'?"

"What's bitten you, Kik'rixk'aq?"

"What's bitten you, Kik're?"

The mosquito returned with the names of all the Lords of Xib'alb'a.

The boys went on their way and finally reached the spot where the lords sat.

"Greet the lords," a lord said.

"The first and second are wooden puppets, not lords," the twins replied. Then they stood in front of the third lord and began greeting them in order.

"Hello, Jun Kame! Hello, Wuqub' Kame! Hello Xikiripat! Hello..." they went around greeting all the lords by name.

The Lords of Xib'alb'a sensed they were losing. "Please sit down and rest."

"This is not a seat for us. That is a burning stone," the boys answered.

They were not to be fooled as were their fathers.

The Tests of Xib'alb'a

Then the lords locked the twins in the Dark House. This was the first test.

"Here's your cigar and your ocote torch. Light them up during the night and tomorrow at daybreak you will return them back to us whole," the messengers told them.

"Very well," answered the boys. They did not light the torch. Instead, they put macaw tail feathers on the tips of the ocote. Thus they appeared red and ablaze in the darkness. They put fireflies at the ends of their cigars so it seemed as if they were smoking them.

In the morning, they returned the cigars and the ocote torches whole. This greatly angered the Lords of Xib'alb'a. They questioned the boys as to their origins and as to who gave birth to them. The twins kept their secret.

"Very well. Let's go play ball," said the Lords of Xib'alb'a.

"Fine, let's play," the boys replied.

The Lords of Xib'alb'a tossed the ball through the boys' hoop and then wanted to kill them with their flint knives.

"Why do you want to kill us? Didn't you just invite us here to play against you?"

"Very well. We will continue playing with your ball," said the lords.

This time the boys tossed the ball through the lords' hoop and the game came to an end. The Lords of Xib'alb'a thought up another test for the boys.

"Early tomorrow morning you will bring to us four gourds filled with flowers," said the Lords of Xib'alb'a.

"What kind of flowers should we bring?" the boys asked.

"We want a bouquet of red chipilín, a bouquet of white chipilín and a yellow chipilín bouquet," said the Lords of Xib'alb'a. They were sure they would triumph over the boys.

The twins were locked in the Knife House, which is the second house of torture in Xib'alb'a. The lords wanted the knives to tear them to pieces, but the boys did not die. They told the knives, "You will only be permitted to cut animal flesh." And the knives did not move.

This is how the boys survived the night in the Knife House. Then they summoned the ants. "You there, black ants and army ants! Go gather together all the flowers that we need for the lords."

"Very well," said the black ants and the army ants, and they went off to cut the flowers in the Lords of Xib'alb'a's gardens. Jun Kame and Wuqub' Kame had warned their sentries to keep a watchful eye on their flowers all through the night. But the sentries did not notice that the black ants and the army ants were cutting flowers. The ants worked, transporting the flowers until they filled the four huge baskets that Jun Kame had ordered.

At daybreak the baskets filled with flowers were presented to Jun Kame and Wuqub' Kame. The Lords of Xib'alb'a grew even angrier at seeing the flowers.

The following night the boys were locked up in the Ice House. But they did not die because they started fires with old logs and held off the cold. The Lords of Xib'alb'a were angrier still and put the boys in the Jaguar House.

The twins spoke to the jaguars. "Don't eat us. We have what you like to eat." And they threw bones to the jaguars, who crushed them with their teeth and ate them. The following day the boys walked out alive from the Jaguar House.

They were thrown into the Fire House, but here also they did not die. Instead, they simply stoked the fire with kindling and spent a warm, toasty night.

Last of all, the lords threw them into the Bat House. This was Kamalotz the vampire bat's hut, which no one could walk out of alive.

The twins defended themselves well and slept inside their blowguns. The bats fluttered about them all night, crying, "Kilitz, kilitz." Suddenly the bats quieted down and all was still. They were clinging to the opening of one of the blowguns.

"Has the sun risen yet?" Ixb'alanke asked.

"Maybe. I'll go out and see," said Junajpu. When he stuck out his head to see if the sun had risen, Kamalotz cut off his head.

"Has the sun risen yet?" Ixb'alanke asked again. When Junajpu did not answer, he realized that his head had been lopped off.

The Lords of Xib'alb'a were overjoyed and hung Junajpu's head in the ball court.

Before daybreak, Ixb'alanke asked all the animals for their help. He called the pizote, the wild hog and all the other creatures, both large and small. Then he told them what they must eat. Last to come was the turtle, for he would take the place of Junajpu's head. Day was about to break and the helpers sent by the Heart of Heaven to aid Ixb'alanke had not finished carving Junajpu's head from the turtle's shell. Finally the head was finished and it was placed on Junajpu's body. Then Ixb'alanke told a rabbit to go into a tomato patch by the ball court.

"Go hide in there. When the ball comes near you, grab it and run. I'll do the rest," Ixb'alanke told the rabbit.

As the sun was rising, the boys approached the ball court. The Lords of Xib'alb'a were certain that they would defeat the boys and so they tossed the ball at the hoop. But the ball sailed over it and landed exactly where the rabbit was hiding. The rabbit grabbed the ball and scurried through the tomato patch. Seeing this, the Lords of Xib'alb'a ran after the rabbit to get the ball back.

Ixb'alanke took advantage of this to bring down Junajpu's real head and put it on his body. Then he hung the turtle shell where Junajpu's real head had been. The boys were overjoyed and continued playing to a tie. When Ixb'alanke threw the ball at the turtle-shell head, it burst into pieces and fell to the ground. And that is how the Lords of Xib'alb'a were defeated.

The Death and Resurrection of Junajpu and Ixb'alanke

NOW WE WILL TELL THE STORY of how Junajpu and Ixb'alanke died. The Lords of Xib'alb'a were so angry that they decided to toss the twins into a bonfire. Knowing that they would die, Junajpu and Ixb'alanke called Xulu' and Paq'am, two seers and wise old men.

"The lords will ask you which is the best way to destroy our bodies. You will tell them that our bones should be crushed and the dust thrown into the river."

The Lords of Xib'alb'a built the fire and invited the boys to drink with them. But Junajpu and Ixb'alanke told them that they knew what they had in mind and so they threw themselves together into the fire. All the Lords of Xib'alb'a shouted happily, "Finally, we have defeated them!"

Afterwards they called the wise men and asked them what they should do with the bones. The wise old men replied that their bones should be ground and then sprinkled over the river's waters.

The lords did this, but the bone dust settled on the river bottom and the two boys were revived. On the fifth day they reappeared and were seen by the people in the water. To the Lords of Xib'alb'a they resembled fish-men.

The following day they appeared as beggars to the people of Xib'alb'a. The only thing these beggars could do was the pujuy or owl dance, the k'u'x or weasel dance, the ib'oy or armadillo dance, and the chitik or the stilt dance. They also performed amazing feats that astonished the people. They would set fire to the huts, which seemed to burn down, but they would soon return to normal without a trace of being burned. They would kill themselves and then come back to life. The people of Xib'alb'a looked upon them with admiration.

So the Lords of Xib'alb'a called forth these beggars who performed marvelous feats. But the beggars refused to appear before the lords, as they were too dirty and tattered. The messengers took them to the Lords of Xib'alb'a by force.

"We want you to dance before us. Burn down our houses and rebuild them at once. We truly admire the amazing things that you can do," said the Lords of Xib'alb'a.

The beggars danced before the lords who watched them, delighted.

"Kill my dog and then bring it back to life," said Jun Kame.

The beggars killed the dog and brought it back to life. The dog wagged its tail, happy to be alive again.

"Burn down my hut and rebuild it at once," Jun Kame ordered.

The beggars did this and the lords were astonished, since they were inside the hut and felt nothing as it burned.

"Kill a man and then bring him back to life," Jun Kame commanded.

The beggars killed a man and then brought him back to life. The Lords of Xib'alb'a were completely astonished.

"Now we want you two to sacrifice one another!"

"Very well," said the beggars, and Ixb'alanke sacrificed Junajpu. Then he brought his twin back to life. The Lords of Xib'alb'a were fascinated, and Jun Kame and Wuqub' Kame said, "Do the same to us. Sacrifice us, tear us to pieces one by one."

"Very well. We will make sure you enjoy yourselves as much as possible," said the beggars.

First they killed Jun Kame, who was the chief Lord of Xib'alb'a, and cut him to pieces. Then they grabbed Wuqub' Kame and did the same. But the two beggars, who were actually Junajpu and Ixb'alanke in disguise, did not want to bring them back to life. The other Lords of Xib'alb'a fled and hid themselves in the deepest ravines. In this way, through marvelous tricks, Junajpu and Ixb'alanke defeated the Lords of Xib'alb'a.

Then they revealed their true identities to the people of Xib'alb'a.

"We are Junajpu and Ixb'alanke. You killed our father here in Xib'alb'a."

The people of Xib'alb'a fell to their knees and asked the boys for forgiveness. The boys felt pity for them and did not kill them. They only told them what they must do.

"Very well," said the boys. "From now on, you will no longer control the ball game. Your domain will be the sinners, the corrupt, the despondent, the wretched and the depraved. You won't be able to take advantage of people so easily."

And this is how the people of Xib'alb'a lost their greatness and were no longer like gods. All they could do was cause evil, sin and discord.

In the meantime, the grandmother wept to see the corn stalks planted in the center of the hut wither as soon as the twins were burned in Xib'alb'a. But she grew happy to see them revive when the boys were brought back to life. And then the boys went to pay tribute to the site where their father, Jun Junajpu, and Wuqub' Junajpu had been killed.

"Your names will not be forgotten and we will invoke your name at dawn," said the twins as they were about to leave Xib'alb'a.

They climbed up to the light of the earth and immediately they rose into the sky. Junajpu became the sun and Ixb'alanke the moon. The four hundred boys also rose to the sky and became stars. And this is how light spread over the sky's vault and over the surface of the earth, for all this happened before man was created and before he walked on the earth.

PART THREE
THE CREATION
OF THE MEN OF CORN

● ● ●

The Third Creation of Humans: The Corn People

WE WILL NOW RETURN TO THE STORY of man's creation by the Creators and Makers Tepew and Q'uk'umatz.

"The time for the first dawn has arrived, and we must complete our creation. Let man and all of humanity appear on the earth's surface. Humankind will give us our sustenance," they said.

They came together in the darkness to think and reflect. This is how they came to decide on the right material for the creation of man. They had to hurry because there was little time left before the sun, the moon and the stars would appear in the sky.

The corn used to create the first men was found in the place called Paxil and K'ayala'. Yak the wildcat, Utiw the coyote, K'el the parrot and Joj the crow, were the creatures who discovered this food. They were the ones who showed the way to Paxil so that the corn could be brought back.

And that is how the beautiful place where abundant white and yellow corn grew was discovered. All kinds of fruits and seeds, including beans, cacao, zapote, anona, wild plums, nance, white zapote and honey were also to be found in Paxil and K'ayala'.

Then our Makers Tepew and Q'uk'umatz began discussing the creation of our first mother and father. Their flesh was made of white and yellow corn. The arms and legs of the four men were made of corn meal. Then Grandmother Ixmukane ground the white and yellow ears of corn to make enough gruel to fill nine gourds to provide strength, muscle and power to the four new men.

The names of the first four men were, in order, B'alam Ki'tze', B'alam Aq'ab', Majukutaj and Iq' B'alam. Only a miracle could have made the first fathers out of white and yellow corn. These first men could speak, hear

and see, and they had enough feeling in their hands to clutch things. They were blessed with intelligence and could see for miles around. From where they stood, they could see all of the sky's vault and the curving surface of the earth. They did not need to move to see what was going on off in the distance.

Then the Creators and Makers asked, "What do you think about your situation? Now can you see everything created on this earth?"

As soon as they saw all the things on earth, they began to thank the Creators and Makers. "We are truly grateful to you, many times over, O, Creator and Maker. We've been created with a mouth and a face. We can speak, hear, think and walk. We can grasp objects and recognize those things both near and far from us. We can also see the big and little things in the sky and the four corners of the earth. We give you our thanks, O, Creator and Maker, for the life you have given us."

But the Creators and Makers were troubled by this response and came together again.

"What our creations tell us—that they can see the big and little things in the sky and on the earth—is not good. What are we going to do with them? Let their vision cloud up a little bit and not allow them to see so far. They cannot possess our powers. They are not gods like us to see everything clearly in the sky and on the earth." This is what the Heart of Heaven, Tepew, Q'uk'umatz, Grandfather Ixpiyakok and Grandmother Ixmukane said.

Then the Heart of Heaven threw a mist over the men's eyes, and their vision blurred as when one breathes on a mirror. From then on, they could only see what was near to them and their eyes could no longer see what was far off. This is how the wisdom and knowledge of the four created men and all their descendants were destroyed.

Then the Creators and Makers decided to make wives for the first four men. While the men slept at night, four beautiful women were placed beside them. When they awoke, they saw their wives and their hearts filled with joy.

Kaja' Paluma' is the wife of B'alam Ki'tze', Chomija' is the wife of B'alam Aq'ab', Tz'ununija' is Majukutaj's wife, and K'aqixaja' is Iq' B'alam's wife.

These were the wives of the four original fathers who multiplied and gave birth to all the small and large tribes of the K'iche' nation.

Many tribes were formed there in the East. Among the most important were the Tepew Oloman, Kojaj, Tamub' and Ilokab'. B'alam Ki'tze' was the grandfather and father of the Kawek. B'alam Aq'ab' was the grandfather and father of the Nijaib'. Majukutaj was the grandfather and father of the Ajaw K'iche'.

Other tribes also followed, among them the Tekpan, the Rabinales, the Kaqchikeles, the Aj Tz'ikinaja', Sajajib', Lamaqib', Kumatz, Tujalja, Uchab'aja, Aj Chuwila', Aj K'ib'aja', Aj B'atenab', Akul Winaq, B'alam Ija, Kanchajeleb' and the B'alam Kolob'. Many more came along, but we will not write down their names.

Many nations were created and multiplied in the East. There were dark-skinned and white-skinned people, all classes of people who spoke different languages. There were people who lived only in the forest and had no homes.

In the beginning they shared one language and all remembered the words of the Creator and Maker. They were gathered together there awaiting the dawn, imploring the Heart of Heaven and the Heart of Earth for offspring. "O, Heart of Heaven and Heart of Earth, do not forsake us! Let us be fruitful and multiply. Give us many level and safe fields and let our people have much peace and happiness. Let us live long lives and useful existences on this earth. Let the sun rise and daybreak appear!"

This is what they said as they waited for the sun to rise and looked upon Venus, the bright morning star.

The Gift of Fire

B'ALAM KI'TZE', B'ALAM AQ'AB', MAJUKUTAJ AND IQ' B'ALAM grew weary of waiting for the sun to rise. Since many tribes had already come along, they went to a place known as Tulan Suiwa to seek their symbols and find their protectors. Each leader accepted an idol as his protector. B'alam Ki'tze' took Tojil, B'alam Aq'ab' took Awilix, Majukutaj took

Jakawitz and Iq' B'alam took Nikatakaj as his god. When they reached Tulan, the language shared by all the tribes was lost, and they could no longer understand one another.

None of the tribes had fire and they were dying from the cold. So the people of B'alam Ki'tze' and B'alam Aq'ab' said to their idols, "O, Tojil and Awilix, we have no fire and we are dying from the cold."

"Do not worry, for I will give you the fire that you need," Tojil replied.

B'alam Ki'tze' and B'alam Aq'ab' were pleased with the fire Tojil gave them. But a huge downpour followed, putting out the fires of all the tribes. Once more B'alam Ki'tze' and B'alam Aq'ab' asked Tojil for fire and again he gave it to them as a gift. But the other tribes were freezing to death. They came to ask B'alam Ki'tze', B'alam Aq'ab', Majukutaj and Iq' B'alam for fire, but they were not well received.

Then all the tribes were sad because they couldn't understand one another. "Ay, we have lost the language we shared. We spoke only one tongue when we came to Tulan. How were we deceived?"

Then a messenger with bat-like wings came from Xib'alb'a. "Don't give the others fire until they've paid tribute to Tojil," said the messenger to B'alam Ki'tze', B'alam Aq'ab', Majukutaj and Iq' B'alam. And then it disappeared.

Very soon the other tribes came to ask B'alam Ki'tze', B'alam Aq'ab', Majukutaj and Iq' B'alam for fire.

"Have pity on us. Give us some of your fire. We are dying from the cold."

So the leaders asked Tojil to reveal his will. The god replied that he would give fire to the tribes if they bowed down and were willing to be sacrificed to him, Tojil, the god of the K'iche'.

The tribesmen were dying from the cold, so they responded, "Very well. We need fire." So they were given fire and warmed themselves. Only one tribe refused to accept Tojil's conditions, and they stole some of the fire. These were the Kaqchikeles, whose god resembled a bat—that's why they are called the Sotz'il. The other tribes, however, began sacrificing themselves to Tojil in return for having received the fire.

Then all the tribes left Tulan. It is not known for sure how they crossed the ocean to return to the land of their origins. It's believed that they walked over long rows of stone when the sea parted. Their journey was filled with great hardships until they reached Chi Pixab' Mountain where they fasted. Then they hid their gods in caves and mountains, since the sun was about to rise. B'alam Ki'tze', B'alam Aq'ab', Majukutaj and Iq' B'alam waited on the peak of Jakawitz Mountain for the sun to rise. That mountain was named for the idol Jakawitz, which was hidden on it.

•

At last day broke and the sun, moon and stars appeared. First to appear was the morning star Venus, and the K'iche', filled with joy, began burning incense. Then the sun rose up and all the animals, both large and small, and the people, too, were happy. The K'eletzu bird was the first to sing, and the puma and jaguar roared good-naturedly. The eagle and the turkey vulture king spread their wings to warm themselves now that the sun had come up.

Before the sun actually appeared, the earth was damp and mushy. But when the sun lit up the earth's surface, the ground began to dry, for the sun's heat was unbearably strong. So Tojil, Awilix, Jakawitz and all the ferocious animals were turned into stones by the sun's heat.

When B'alam Ki'tze', B'alam Aq'ab', Majukutaj and Iq' B'alam went to visit their idols, they found them miraculously transformed into young men. These gods asked their worshippers to sustain them with offerings of incense, birds and deer. The idol Nikatakaj did not appear again.

PART FOUR
THE FIRST FATHERS OF
THE K'ICHE' NATION

● ● ● ●

The Founding of the Tribes

MANY TRIBES CAME TOGETHER and gathered together near the foot-paths. Meanwhile, B'alam Ki'tze', B'alam Aq'ab', Majukutaj and Iq' B'alam headed for the mountains and could not be seen. Whenever one or two people came down the path, the first four men would howl like coyotes and wildcats. They also roared like pumas and jaguars from somewhere in the jungle.

"They're pretending they are not human just to trick us. They only want to get rid of us," said the members of the other tribes.

Then B'alam Ki'tze', B'alam Aq'ab', Majukutaj and Iq' B'alam came before Tojil, Awilix and Jakawitz to make them an offering of birds and deer. They also pricked their ears to give blood to their gods. Tojil, Jakawitz and Awilix disguised themselves as boys and began to ask for tributes of blood.

And this is why B'alam Ki'tze', B'alam Aq'ab', Majukutaj and Iq' B'alam abducted men. When one or two of them were off walking, they would seize them and sacrifice them. Then they'd sprinkle their blood on the path, leaving the head a good distance from the body. Thus began the kidnapping and death of people who walked alone along the roads.

"A jaguar attacked them," said the people, seeing the tracks on the ground.

Many men had been abducted before the people realized they were being fooled.

"So many men are dying because Tojil, Awilix and Jakawitz must be asking for human sacrifice. Where's their house? Let's follow their trail," said the tribes.

So the tribes held counsel. The people and their leaders said, "Let us all

---

rise up, let us call the others, let no one amongst all the tribes stay behind."

When they were all gathered together they asked themselves, "How can we defeat the K'iche' of Kawek who are killing our sons? Do we not have enough men among us?"

Some said they had seen Tojil, Jakawitz, and Awilix bathing every day in the river.

"If it is they who are bathing then we must overcome them first. Then we can defeat B'alam Ki'tze', B'alam Aq'ab', Majukutaj and Iq' B'alam, because they will no longer have protectors," they said.

"But how will we defeat them?" some asked.

"Let's send two beautiful maidens to wash clothes in the river. Then they can seduce Tojil, Jakawitz and Awilix," said the leaders of the tribes.

They picked out the most beautiful young girls from among their daughters and said, "Go to the river to do the washing. If you see some boys, take off your clothes to attract them. If they ask who you are, tell them that you are daughters of noblemen. Then ask them for something you can bring us as a sign. If they desire you, surrender to their wishes, but bring us something as proof that you have fulfilled our request."

This is what they said to Ixtaj and Ixpuch', the two beautiful maidens sent on this mission.

The two girls went to wash by the river. As soon as they had taken off their clothes, Tojil, Awilix and Jakawitz came along. But they felt no desire.

"Why have you come to this river where we bathe?" Tojil asked.

"The nobles of the tribes sent us to gaze upon your faces. They commanded us to return with proof that we had seen you," they replied.

"Very well. We'll send them proof that you have seen us," said Tojil.

Then Tojil told B'alam Ki'tze', B'alam Aq'ab' and Majukutaj to paint four capes for the maidens. Iq' B'alam would not paint a cape. B'alam Ki'tze' painted a jaguar on his, B'alam Aq'ab' an eagle, and Majukutaj wasps and horseflies on his. The capes were then taken to the two maidens in the river.

"Here's proof that you talked to Tojil. Take these capes to the noblemen of the tribes so that they may wear them," said B'alam Ki'tze', B'alam Aq'ab' and Majukutaj.

The maidens went back with the capes and the noblemen were pleased.

"Have you seen the faces of Tojil, Awilix and Jakawitz?"

"Yes, we have seen them," the maidens replied, spreading out the capes painted with jaguars, eagles and wasps. The paintings were so fabulous that the noblemen wanted to wear them.

So the head nobleman put on the cape painted with jaguars and nothing happened. Then he tried on the eagle cape and nothing happened. But when he put on the cape with the horseflies and wasps, they began stinging him all over his body. The nobleman howled in pain from the stings of the wasps Majukutaj had painted on the cape.

And this is how B'alam Ki'tze', B'alam Aq'ab', Majukutaj and Iq' B'alam defeated the tribes and their noble leaders.

The tribes once more held counsel and agreed to destroy B'alam Ki'tze', B'alam Aq'ab', Majukutaj and Iq' B'alam.

"We shall arm ourselves with bows, arrows and shields and defeat them. Not one, not two of us shall remain behind the others," said the noble leaders.

Once again the tribes regrouped to attack B'alam Ki'tze', B'alam Aq'ab', Majukutaj and Iq' B'alam, who had settled at the top of Jakawitz Mountain. They had raised a fortress wall around their city and had carved puppets that they placed atop the wall. These puppets resembled men because they were suited up and held spears and shields in their hands. B'alam Ki'tze' asked Tojil if they were going to be routed by the enemy.

"Don't worry. Nothing will happen as long as I am with you," Tojil said. They went off to catch wasps and horseflies, which they placed in four huge pots at each corner of the fortress wall. Then they hid themselves. As the tribe scouts neared, they saw that the wall was defended by a small number of warriors, which from a distance seemed to be men but were actually puppets.

B'alam Ki'tze', B'alam Aq'ab', Majukutaj and Iq' B'alam were all together hiding on the mountain with their wives and children when the warriors arrived. More warriors than could be counted came to the foot of the mountain whistling and shouting. They were just about to storm the city when the four large pots with the hidden wasps and horseflies were uncovered. The insects took off like smoke and attacked the warriors as they climbed up the foothills. They drove their stingers right into the warriors' eyes and stung their faces, ears and noses. Thus the warriors were defeated by poisonous insects. Even the wives of B'alam Ki'tze', B'alam Aq'ab', Majukutaj and Iq' B'alam rushed out to charge and kill the warriors, who had fallen unconscious to the ground from the wasp bites.

"Have pity on us, don't kill us," the warriors begged. And this is how the tribes surrendered and became vassals to the K'iche'.

The Death of the First Fathers

NOW WE WILL TELL YOU how B'alam Ki'tze', B'alam Aq'ab', Majukutaj and Iq' B'alam died.

B'alam Ki'tze' had two sons, Kokawib' and Kokab'ib'. B'alam Aq'ab' also had two sons, Ko'akul and Ko'akutek. Majukutaj had only one son, Ko'ajaw. Iq' B'alam had no sons or descendants.

When these first four fathers realized they were about to die, they advised their sons, "Dear ones, it is time for us to go but we will leave you wise guidance and counsel. Since we have accomplished our mission, we must now return from where we came. Think of us and never forget us. You will see your homes and your mountains once more. Settle down there and be fruitful and multiply."

Then B'alam Ki'tze' left a sign of his presence among his people. This was a bundle known as P'isom Q'aq'al, whose contents were invisible. And this is how the first four fathers disappeared there atop Jakawitz Mountain where their children remained.

This is how the Kawek people originated. They kept guard of the bundle that B'alam Ki'tze' had left them as a sign that he was always among them.

After the death of their fathers, Kokab'ib', Ko'akutek and Ko'ajaw decided to go to the East where their fathers had come from. They crossed the sea and went to visit the great lord Nakxit, who gave them the banners and the paintings they brought back from Tulan. The people were pleased when Kokab'ib', Ko'akutek and Ko'ajaw returned to their tribes after such a long journey. Shortly thereafter, the wives of B'alam Ki'tze', B'alam Aq'ab', Majukutaj and Iq' B'alam also died atop Jakawitz Mountain.

Then the survivors left Jakawitz and looked for other places to settle. They founded the city of Chi K'ix, but soon left to settle in other areas and build new cities.

And this is how they founded the city of Chi Ismachi', where they lived in peace. They were not at war, for only happiness resided in their hearts. But soon, the Ilokab' people rose up against Kotuja, the K'iche' king. But King Kotuja captured them and they were forced to serve the K'iche'. And so the wars began and the K'iche' ruled over the other tribes once the three huge nations of Kawek, Nijaib' and Ilokab' joined them. And they searched for their wives from among these tribes.

After abandoning Chi Ismachi', they came to another place where they founded the city of Q'umarkaj. This was now the fifth generation of men from the time they were given birth by the first four mothers and fathers. In Q'umarkaj they split off again, since their tribes no longer intermarried. The city grew large, and its people divided themselves into twenty-four families or lineages.

The greatness of the K'iche' nation grew, thanks to the workings of King Q'uk'umatz, who could transform himself into a jaguar, an eagle or a snake. At other times he became dried blood. All the other nations and noblemen feared him, as he was such a powerful king. Q'uk'umatz transformed himself into all kinds of animals to show his power and to be able to rule the people.

King K'iq'ab' came to power thereafter and he also was very powerful and was part of the seventh generation. The people began to detest K'iq'ab' when this king enslaved the other nations and forced them to pay tribute taxes.

Q'uk'umatz, Kotuja, K'iq'ab' and Kawisimaj were very powerful kings. They knew when it was time to go to war and when there would be famine or slaughter. They were very wise men, for they foresaw all this in a book they called the *Popol Vuh*. The kings also fasted and always prayed to Tojil, asking for the happiness of their sons and daughters.

"O, you, beauty of day! O, you, Heart of Heaven and Heart of Earth! You the giver of life, the giver of sons and daughters! Give life to our children and let them be fruitful and multiply. Let them not find danger either in front or behind them. Give them safe paths and do not let them have misfortunes, but much happiness instead. Let those who nourish you have a bountiful existence, O, Heart of Heaven and Heart of Earth!"

One, alone, was the source for the traditions and customs of all nations.

The Genealogy of the K'ichc' Kings

NOW YOU SHALL LEARN of the descendants of the first four fathers, B'alam Ki'tze', B'alam Aq'ab', Majukutaj and Iq' B'alam.

B'alam Ki'tze': The first man created. The root of the Kawek K'iche'.
Kokawib' and Kokab'ib': second generation
B'alam K'onache: third generation
Kotuja and Istayub': fourth generation
Q'uk'umatz and Kotuja: fifth generation and the beginning of the powerful kings
Tepepul and Istayub': sixth generation
K'iq'ab' and Kawisimaj: seventh generation
Tepepul and Istayub': eighth generation
Tekum and Tepepul: ninth generation
Wajxaqib' K'am and K'iq'ab': tenth generation
Wuqub' Noj and Ka'utepech: eleventh generation
Oxib' Kej and B'elejeb' Tzi: twelfth generation—these were the rulers when Tonatiuj (Pedro de Alvarado, the Spaniard who conquered Guatemala) came; they were strangled by the Spaniards
Tekum and Tepepul: thirteenth generation (they gave their allegiance to the Spaniards)
Don Juan de Rojas and Don Juan Cortés: fourteenth generation

B'alam Aq'ab': The second man created. The root of the Nijaib' K'iche'.

Ko'akul and Ko'akutek: second generation

Kochahu and Kotzibaha': third generation

B'elejeb' Kej [I]: fourth generation

Kotuja [I]: fifth generation

B'atz'a: sixth generation

Istayub': seventh generation

Kotuja [II]: eighth generation

B'elejeb' Kej [II]: ninth generation

Kema': tenth generation

Ajaw Kotuja: eleventh generation

Don Cristobal: twelfth generation, ruled during the Spanish Conquest

Don Pedro de Robles: thirteenth generation

Majukutaj: The third man created. The root of the Ajaw K'iche'.

Ko'ajaw: second generation

Kaqlaqan: third generation

Kokosom: fourth generation

Komajkun: fifth generation

Wuqub' Aj: sixth generation

Kokamel: seventh generation

Koyabakoj: eighth generation

Winaq B'am: ninth generation

Iq' B'alam: The fourth man created. No descendants.

This is the ancient history of the Maya K'iche' written down in the *Popol Vuh*. This book existed in ancient times but has been lost and these stories can no longer be read. Now we have written them down so that the history of the ancient kings and their descendants who still live in the town now called Santa Cruz del Quiché will be known.

Glossary

The transliteration of K'iche' words follows the most recent rules laid down by la Academia de las lenguas Mayas (the Academy of Maya Languages) which is based in Guatemala. The j should be read in English as though it were an h. In Guatemala, today, the book is often called *Pop Wuj*. The traditional name has been retained for this version because it is more familiar.

In the original *Popol Vuh* there are some inconsistencies in the names and features of some beings. For example, Heart of Heaven, Heart of Earth is sometimes simply referred to as Heart of Heaven. The idol Nikatakaj suddenly disappears without explanation. The author has followed the original in such cases.

GODS

Awilix: idol that B'alam Aq'ab' brought back from Tulan; he sometimes appears as a young man

Heart of Heaven, Heart of Earth: poetic name of God

Jakawitz: idol that Majukutaj brought back from Tulan; a mountain is named after him; he sometimes appears as a young man

Juraqan: name of God

Ixmukane: first grandmother, a mythic ancestor

Ixpiyakok: first grandfather, a mythic ancestor

Ixtoj, Ixq'anil, Ixkakaw: goddesses of agriculture

Nakxit: great lord of Tulan to whom the first fathers went to get their signs and idols

Nikatakaj: idol that Iq' B'alam brought back from Tulan; he does not reappear after the sun turned him to stone

Q'uk'umatz: one of the Creators and Makers; the plumed serpent; he had quetzal feathers

Saqi Nim Ak', Saqi Nima Tz'i': names given to the Creator and Maker when they appear as an old man and an old woman

Tepew: one of the Creators and Makers

Tojil: idol that B'alam Ki'tze' brought back from Tulan; he sometimes appears as a young man

---

DEMI-GODS

Chimalmat: mythic woman, Wuqub' K'aqix's wife

Chitik: ancient dance on stilts

Ixb'alanke: one of the amazing twins; son of Jun Junajpu and Ixkik'; twin of Junajpu; has jaguar skin patches on his body

Ixkik': daughter of Kuchumakik' and mother of the amazing twins

Junajpu: one of the amazing twins; son of Jun Junajpu and Ixkik'; twin of Ixb'alanke; has spots on his skin

Jun B'atz': one of Jun Junajpu's elder sons, whose name means monkey

Jun Ch'owem: one of Jun Junajpu's elder sons, the one who puts things in order

Jun Junajpu: one of the first set of twins; father of the amazing twins; twin brother of Wuqub' Junajpu; his name means blowgun

Kab'raqan: Wukub K'aqix's second son, meaning one who topples mountains

Sipakna: Wuqub' K'aqix's first son, the giant who claimed he created the mountains

Tizate: white substance similar to chalk, used by the twins to defeat Kab'raqan

Wuqub' Junajpu: one of the first set of twins; uncle to the amazing twins; twin brother of Jun Junajpu

Wuqub' K'aqix: Lord "Seven Macaws," who believed he was the sun and the moon; father of Sipakna and Kab'raqan

Xulu' and Paq'am: two wisemen and seers who advised the Lords of Xib'alb'a to crush the bones of Junajpu and Ixb'alanke and throw them into the river

XIB'ALB'A

Ajalk'ana': lord of Xib'alb'a, lord of the fever

Ajalmes: lord of Xib'alb'a who caused heart attacks and sudden death

Ajalpuj: lord of Xib'alb'a, lord of the pus-filled sore

Ajaltoq'ob': lord of Xib'alb'a, the one who caused suffering, caused heart attacks and sudden death

Chamiyab'aq: lord of Xib'alb'a, lord of the bones, the one who made people thin

Chamiyajom: lord of Xib'alb'a, Chamiyab'aq's companion, the skeleton lord

Jun Kame: chief lord of Xib'alb'a, whose name means Lord Death

Kik'xik': lord of Xib'alb'a, companion to Patan

Kik're: lord of Xib'alb'a, companion to Kik'rixk'aq

Kik'rixk'aq: lord of Xib'alb'a, companion to Kik're

Kuchumakik': lord of Xib'alb'a who made people vomit blood; his name means joined bloodlines; father of Princess Ixkik'

Lords of Xib'alb'a: lords living in the Underworld who brought on various illnesses to the humans living on the earth

Patan: lord of Xib'alb'a, companion to Kik'xik'; caused accidents on roadways

Wuqub' Kame: second most important lord of Xib'alb'a

Xib'alb'a: Underworld, the place of fear, where the amazing twins went to play ball

Xikiripat: lord of Xib'alb'a who made people vomit blood

HUMAN WORLD

B'alam Aq'ab': second man created from corn

B'alam Ki'tze': first man created from corn

Chicha: alcoholic drink made from fermenting corn

Chomija': wife of B'alam Aq'ab', one of the first women created

Holi, holi, huki, huki: the sound that a grinding stone makes when it breaks up and grinds corn

Iq' B'alam: fourth man created from corn

Ixpuch' and Ixtaj: the girls sent to the river to seduce Tojil, Jakawitz and Awilix

Kaja' Paluma': B'alam Ki'tze's wife; one of the first four women created

Kaqixaja': Iq' B'alam's wife; one of the first four women created

Kaqchikeles: Guatemalan Mayan nation; according to the *Popol Vuh* they emigrated with the K'iche'

K'iche': Guatemalan Mayan nation; descendants of the ancient Maya whose language is K'iche'

Kojaj: allies of the K'iche' who came from the East

Majukutaj: third man created from corn

P'isom Q'aq'al: the bundle B'alam Ki'tze' left for his people and whose contents were invisible

Popol Vuh: Today often called *Pop Wuj*, it is the sacred book of the Maya K'iche', also known as the Book of Counsels; pop means power or sacred; wuj means paper or book

Tepew Olomanes: the Olmecs, who lived in Veracruz, México

Tz'ununija': Majukutaj's wife and one of the first women created

ANIMALS

Ib'oy: armadillo

Ixmukur: forest dove

Joj: crow

Kamalotz: vampire bat

K'el: parrot

K'eletzu: bird that sings at daybreak

Kilitz, kilitz: the sound a bat makes

Kotz'b'alam: jaguar

K'u'x: weasel

Pizote: raccoon-like mammal with a long flexible nose

Pujuy: pygmy owl, or the sound this bird makes at night

Sakikas: snake

Sotz'il: people of sotz', or a bat

Tamasul: toad

Tukum b'alam: puma

Utiw: coyote

Wak: sparrow hawk

Xa'n: mosquito who, by biting the Lords of Xib'alb'a, revealed their names

Xek'otk'owach: vulture or turkey buzzard

Yak: wildcat

PLANTS

Anona: custard apple

Cacao: cocoa, the plant from which chocolate is made

Calabash: a kind of squash

Chik'te': magic plant, its sap thickened in the shape of the heart of Princess Ixkik'

Chipilín: plant with edible leaves used by the Maya; it can make you sleepy

Ek': bromeliad or air plant that grows on tree branches

Ocote: strip of resinous pine wood that is used to light fires or as a torch

Tz'ite': red seed from the coral tree used for divination

Zapote: a fruit

PLACES

Chi Pixab': mountain where the tribesmen fasted

Jakawitz Mountain: mountain named after the god

K'ayala': a place where corn was found

Meaván Mountain: located near the town of Rabinal in northern Guatemala

Motz: Pleiades constellation, meaning crowd

Paxil: a place where corn was found

Q'umarkaj: Mayan name for the ancient K'iche' capital, now known as Santa Cruz del Quiché

Tulan: according to the *Popol Vuh,* the city in the highlands of Guatemala from which the K'iche' people emigrated, also known as Tulan Suiwa, the Tulan Cave